# THE GRASS THAT SUFFERS

Janet Storton

**JUST DUST**
PUBLISHERS

Just Dust Publishers
1025 NE Irvine Street
McMinnville, Oregon 97128
Office@JustDustPublishers.com

© 2014 by Just Dust Publishers
All rights reserved. Published 2014
No part of this book, neither text nor photos,
may be reproduced in any manner without permission
from the publisher. To obtain consent, contact:
office@JustDustPublishers.com
Printed in the United States of America
First paperback edition, 2014
ISBN: 978-0-9838333-7-6

Photographs: Janet Storton
Cover and interior design: Lynn Miller
Author photograph on cover: Lynn Woodward

# THE
# GRASS
# THAT
# SUFFERS

*"When two elephants fight, it is the grass that suffers."*

This Ugandan proverb illustrates the ongoing reality
that when war is waged, it is the powerless,
particularly the children, that suffer
like the grass below the elephants' feet.

## SPECIAL THANKS

*Some are called to step outside the safe and normal life, to pursue our dreams and what we believe in. It was crucial for me to have a large support system. Without my husband, Peter, as a pillar; teams of family and friends; a board of directors advising my path; and my "quilting angels" (all of the women who help with production and sales) all my endeavors would crumble. The reinforcement I received through emails during the stressful days and nights, isolated from the modern world and living in a foreign country under primitive conditions, sustain me. It would be difficult to endure without the support from home. Listening to the heart wrenching stories of men and women burdened with living life under the weight of a rebel war, poverty, and despair, but still loving and praying to their God, inspires me!*

*My warm appreciation to Shelley L. Houston, president of Just Dust Publishers, who took a chance on me and this story and pushed me to tell it so others could know and share my journey. This is to the readers who are interested in learning...the grim and the good in Africa.*

# FORWARD

My eyes welled up with tears as I listened to a young woman's story of being abducted and held captive under the worst conditions imaginable. I felt our conversation had a healing effect as she dug deeply for the details and memories.

When she finished recounting her experiences, I asked her to stand. I wrapped her in an embrace, not wanting to let go, desiring to take away all the hurt and pain she suffered.

I then held her at arms' length and told her, "I'm going to tell your story." The passive look on her face changed to a beaming smile with deeply indented dimples. Telling her I would write her story gave her a sense of calm that eased the pain buried in her heart for over eleven years.

Psalm 102:17 tells us, "He will listen to the prayers of the destitute. He will not reject their pleas." God listened to Stella, I listened, and I knew others needed to hear her story. I have endeavored to write Stella's story in order to give a glimpse into the souls of the girls who have suffered and are now trying to repair their lives. For me, sharing awareness of the brutality of life, as well as the intense beauty, brings healing of my pain after hearing so many experiences like Stella's. My journey is to share these stories so that others will know.

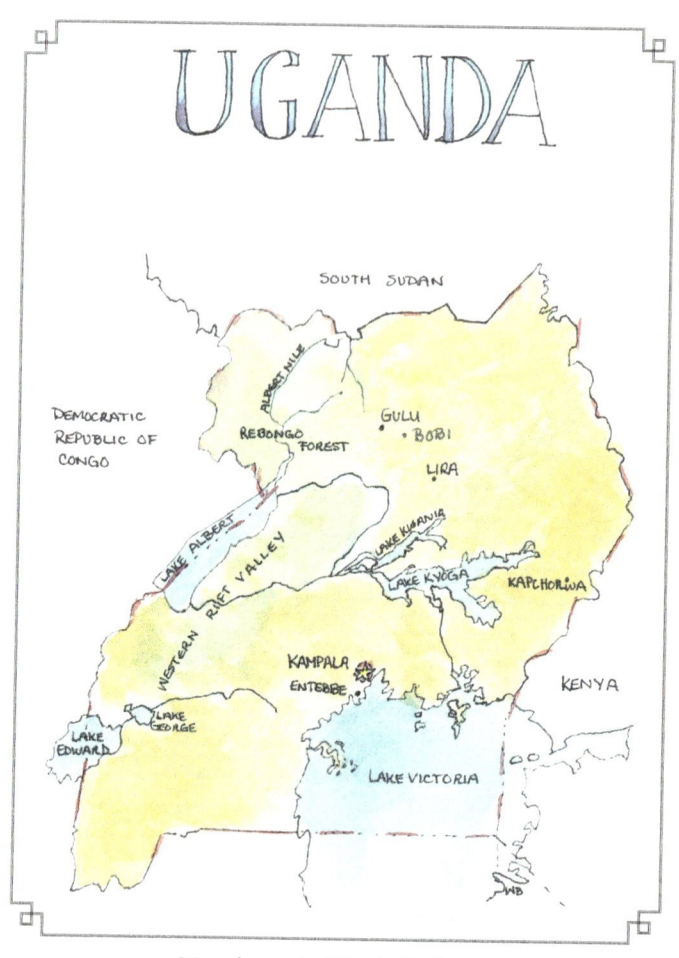

*Map drawn by Wendy Bachmeier*

## Prologue

# 2003
# THE VILLAGE OF BOBI, UGANDA

Lightning bolts collided again and again in the distance. Thunder rolled across the plains, shaking the grass roof above me. I curled close to my sisters on the hard earth floor with only a woven mat underneath and a thin sheet over me to ward off the cold, damp air.

As the thunder grew louder, I was snapped from my dreams and sat up to listen. I began to hear voices, cackling, and war chanting, as the trucks came bounding into my village of Bobi. I peeked out to see rebels waving rifles in the air, and knew they had only death and lust on their minds. When the trucks came to a roaring stop, rebels leaped out of the trucks and began firing into the pitch black sky, ready to begin their rampage. I bolted from my hut knowing the dreaded night raiders had come.

~Stella

1

# A CALLING, EARLY IN LIFE

Mesmerized, I listened to the story of missionaries at our church one Sunday. My ten year old heart was stirred. I returned home and excitedly informed my mother, "One day, I am going to work in Africa!"

As only a loving mother would, she nodded her head and smiled, "Perhaps you will." The seed was planted.

Throughout my youth, I immersed myself in books about stories of people who had stepped out of their comfort zone to travel, reaching the unreached. I read histories of Africa, and novels of intrigue and adventure in foreign countries. I scoured the library for accounts of foreigners colonizing in Africa, which were especially appealing to me. I found books on the Underground Railroad, slaves achieving their freedom, and Africans abducted and forced into the slave trade. I dreamed that one day the desire of my heart would become a reality.

I had been taught by wonderful pastors throughout my Christian education that when God has a plan, you must wait for His timing. Wait I did.

My plans for joining the Peace Corp after college were

derailed when I married Peter, now my husband of 44 years. I found new joys and purpose in life as a mother raising four children, and as owner of an interior design business. My focus was on the lives of my children. Thoughts of traveling and mission work in Africa became a distant memory.

In 2006, I sold my business. My children were grown and starting their own families and careers. I had the time now and could return, once again, to my childhood passion.

I started looking for a volunteer position in Oregon, where I was living, and a door suddenly opened. I found long-forgotten dreams realized.

It was His plan, His timing. And His timing was now mine.

When Paul Rawlins, the director of missions at Sisters Community Church, heard I was looking for volunteer work, he said to me, "Stop looking, Janet. I need you in Africa." My heart stopped. He then asked if I would like to go to Uganda with a medical mission team. He had no knowledge of my long-term desire. My joy was overwhelming.

I left for my first trip to Africa, in 2007, for what I thought would be a once in a lifetime opportunity and a reward for all the reading, longing, and preparing for such a trip. The moment I set foot on African soil, I knew this would not be a one-time visit. As the Bible states in the first sentence of Ecclesiastes 11:5, "As you do not know the path of the wind, or how the body is formed in a mother's womb, so, you cannot understand the work of God, the maker of all things." I knew then the direction that God's wind was taking me.

It would only take a few days before I felt the consuming belief that this is where I was supposed to be. This is where God had led me.

Before leaving home, I had researched Uganda and the areas we would be traveling during this short mission trip. Once I arrived, I had an overwhelming sense that I was completely at home.

I went as a volunteer with a medical team. I am not a nurse. I did not come to teach Bible studies or preach the gospel. I came to help as a lay person, taking temperatures, weighing babies, filling out cards with names of those who needed to see a doctor.

Hundreds were lining up each day, and I was told to go down the lines and look for those I thought needed care the most. I walked along the long lines of those eager to be selected, some who had come from miles away to see the nurse or doctor. It was painful to pass up ones that didn't appear to be ill. Some were only curious to see the Americans. Some had never seen a white person before.

However, I was not unqualified for my position. After raising four children of my own, I could recognize the look in the eyes of a sick child, could feel a fevered brow, or know the panic of a mother wanting the best care for her child. I wondered how any of the mothers slept at night with so many sick with malaria, HIV, or a virus.

Our team went to the most unreached villages where medical care and doctors were unavailable or few. News spread fast that Americans with a medical team were here to help. Conversation from neighbor to neighbor traveled quickly along the hills of Mount Elgon, in eastern Uganda.

*Medical clinic in the mountains*

Each day more who were ill, lame, or pregnant poured

in to see us. Mothers carried feverish babies on their backs. Older children carried the younger ones. The crippled were supported by family members, or hobbled in using large sticks as canes. It was heartbreaking to turn some of them away at the end of the day to make the long trip back home without seeing a doctor. There were not enough doctors to care for the hundreds that came.

On that first trip we visited the village of Kapchorwa, located in the rural hills of Mt. Elgon. Sisters Community Church in Sisters, Oregon, partnered with this village to build a primary school and develop a sponsorship program for children, which provided education and basic needs. It was a natural decision, due to my passion for quilting, to bring a few simple quilts as gifts to two children my husband and I sponsored.

Kapchorwa was to be the last village we would visit after two weeks of providing medical clinics on the move.

During our last evening in Kapchorwa, there was a gathering for us to meet the children we sponsored and their parents or guardians.

Although I knew that the village was located in a mountainous region, I had no idea the quilts were so needed and would be so meaningful to the children. (An account of this exchange and its significance can be read in my first book, *Mercy's Quilt*.)

After presenting the two quilts, I was surrounded by many women of the village. The ladies of Kapchorwa saw that the "blankets of color," as they called them, would keep their children warm on cold rainy nights. They pleaded with me to return and teach them the skill of quilting—something they had never seen before.

That night it became clear to me that I needed to return. I saw that quilting would not only provide warmth for their children, but would also provide vocational training for the women, something they so desperately needed. God decided to utilize my love of sewing and my love of Africa for His purpose, to teach the women in Uganda. I then realized this had all been in His timing and was His plan for me.

None of the difficulties or hardships of living in a third world country had bothered me. I had prepared...I had waited...I was ready!

At the close of that first trip, I climbed the stairs to the airplane on the Entebbe tarmac for the return flight home with a certain hope. I knew in my heart that the dreams of my youth were being fulfilled. The wind was blowing; I would return over and over.

*The farm refugee women learning to quilt*

2

# INTERNALLY
# DISPLACED - PERSONS
# CAMP

My first trip to Gulu, in northern Uganda, was in February of 2008. I traveled with a photographer and his wife, Eli and Kelly Pyke, staying on a refugee farm in Kigumba, just a few hours' drive from Gulu. I was there to instruct the women in basic sewing skills. A mission group had purchased several sewing machines, but there was no teacher. Most of the people who were brought to the farm were rescued from rebel captivity, including young boys who had been turned into child soldiers. Many of the women were widowed, having lost husbands and children to the war or having been held as camp slaves by the rebels.

Eli was making a video of the traumas of being captured by the rebel army. He asked the rescued boys and girls to reenact the experiences they shared for his film. While sitting around a cook fire that evening with some of the women, I jumped up, alarmed at the screaming and crying I heard in the distance. Thinking it was an actual raid, I was ready to run to the commotion. The ladies told me not to fear, the children were acting for the film.

Listening to the cries for help, I could only imagine how I would have felt if they were my own children, crying out, needing to be rescued. That night was the first time I heard some of the individual stories of the atrocities that were occurring in the northern villages. I will never forget the chilling sounds of the screams and what these women, wives, mothers, and captives went through. Looking around me, seeing mostly flat farm land, I wondered to myself where I would hide my children. How could I have survived living with such terror? I felt the impact of the tragedies and what these women went through. Later, when I heard Stella's story, it was easy to imagine what she and her mother endured during the attack on Bobi.

Although rebel groups were known to still be in the northern district, we learned that peace talks were underway. Kony's army leaders and the Ugandan government were gathering in South Sudan. Supported by the United Nations, a counsel from South Sudan would mediate the talks. The raiding activity had come to a standstill due to a cease fire agreement signed while the meetings were being conducted.

The owner of the farm where we were staying, told us he had a cousin and family living in an Internally Displaced Persons (IDP) Camp in Gulu, the dreaded territory of the rebels. We wanted to visit the camps so Eli could film where the war was taking place and some of the people living there. Fearless, we found a driver and headed north. We wanted to see firsthand the people living under these conditions and hear their stories. We could only spend the day, knowing it would not be safe at night.

As we were approaching Gulu, we crossed a bridge over the Nile River. Our cameras came out to take photos of the beauty at this section of the river. Seeing a military patrol standing at the side of the road, the driver told us to quickly put our cameras down in case they were rebels impersonating Ugandan forces. As one of the uniformed men started walking toward our car waving us to stop, the driver took off. He said whether military or rebels, most likely they were coming to confiscate our cameras.

At a place in the road that dipped down into a ravine, the driver told us to slink low in our seats. He sped up, and then informed us that this was where snipers from the rebel army were known to shoot at cars driving through to the camps.

We were relieved when we reached the top of the ravine. However, when we looked across the dry arid savannah, we were shocked by the view. For miles and miles there was a sea of small circular mud huts packed tightly together. I was devastated by the scene and could hardly believe that masses in this quantity could live in such close proximity to each other. We were told two million people were living in these crowded government built compounds. Villagers were brought into these communes with the hope of keeping them safe.

Once again, as we headed towards the mass of huts, we were waved over by military, this time wearing the uniforms of officers. Afraid they would start shooting if he sped off, our driver pulled over and started a conversation with one of the officers in their native language. It was a lengthy conversation, and one we could not understand. I could tell the driver was becoming agitated and involved in an argument with the man. Finally, the officer disgustedly waved him off to continue driving. We asked him what that was about and were told the officer only wanted a ride to one of the camps. With all of our luggage, a mound of photographic gear, and four adults in the small car, the driver kept telling the officer there was no room! The aggravation came when the officer tried to talk him into letting one of us out on this desolate road so the officer could be driven where he wanted to go. He said the driver could come back later to pick up the one left behind. This could have meant a wait of hours and hours in an unsafe environment for the one chosen to stay. We were thankful we had found this brave driver that day.

Once we reached the camp, we found the cousin and his family of five. We went into the small, airless hut to talk to them about the life they were leading after being displaced from their farm. The conditions and squalor the people were living under were horrendous. The wife and daughter walked miles every day bringing water to the family, getting up at 4 a.m. to make this two hour daily ritual.

Large families lived in one windowless hut. Stacks of rocks marked the graves of family members just outside the huts.

*Family graves besides huts in IDP camp*

There was a lack of sanitation and latrines, and, worst of all, a lack of food for the thousands of children living in these camps. My heart was broken as I took pictures of some of the most destitute children I had ever seen.

They were filthy, covered in scabies, shoeless, and wearing tattered and torn clothing. Some had distended stomachs from a lack of food, and orange tinted hair from a lack of nutrition. Yet, as I snapped their photos and turned the camera around so they could see their faces for the first time, I was rewarded with infectious giggles and smiles.

They followed me around like a swarm of bees, excited a Mazungu (white person) had come to take their pictures. We were all distraught by the stories we heard and the conditions in which we found them living. We reluctantly left the oceans of huts behind and headed to a city where we would be safer.

*IDP camp children, Gulu*

Shortly after arriving home in the U.S., I learned from watching the African news on the internet that the peace talks were dissolved without a solution. Joseph Kony refused to appear or sign a peace treaty, claiming to be misled and afraid of being arrested. The rebel commanders walked away from the discussions and went back to the northern Ugandan jungles to once again continue their atrocities. They began raiding the IDP camps, like the one we visited, knowing there would be many children available for abduction. Only a few weeks after I returned to the States, over one thousand children were abducted, mostly from the IDP camps, and added to their ranks. The images captured on my camera that day, of smiling children, are a searing memory of the destitution we found in the camps. The raiding by Kony's rebels continues today in other countries.

3

# OTINO WAA

In 2008, I made my first trip to an orphanage in Lira, southeast of Gulu, called Otino Waa, the Luo word for "our children." In Lira, a large town and raiding grounds for Kony's army, an American couple, Bob and Carol Higgins, developed a school, orphanage, and vocational program for hundreds of rescued boys and girls.

*Otino Waa school in Lira*

Their first visit to Uganda was in 1999, while on a short-term mission trip. They saw the devastation of what was happening in the north and decided to return. They visited a pastor in Lira and found a congregation of children living in the garden of the pastor's house. With a small home, he could not keep them all inside. The children believed just living on the grounds close to him would keep them safe. Bob and Carol learned the children were eating only every few days, living off of what they could steal from other people's gardens. After buying a few bags of beans and blankets for the children, they were convinced there was a greater need than just a bag of beans, and so the school began! They knew without better protection the children would become victims of the rebel raids which were coming closer to this area. Most of the children brought to Bob and Carol's school were rescued captives of the rebel camps or children that had lost parents during the war.

The Higgins lived there for fourteen years, within rebel territory, taking in orphans and devoting their lives to saving these children; giving them a home, education, and hope for a future. It was a privilege for me to be there on a few occasions, getting to know this heroic couple, and helping them with what training I could to assist the students in repairing their damaged lives.

All of the northern towns of Uganda were in the territories ravaged by Joseph Kony's army. It was there

I found people lacking in education. The war had kept it from them for a generation. The years of war had interrupted their lives. A gap widened for the young girl or boy who had a difficult time paying their school fees for an education, until it became almost impossible at an advanced age. It is not easy for a sixteen year old to enter back into the second grade. Educations are usually denied to a girl who has become sexually active, whether or not it was considered rape or abuse, after returning home. For this reason Otino Waa became an important haven for some of the rescued boys and girls.

*Carol Higgins with rescued students*

Over the years, many of the young girls abducted and released would return home with babies or infected with disease. Occasionally, once the girls had given birth, the fear of crying babies giving away their position would bring about their release. But, then the walk to freedom may mean days or weeks without food. In addition, the threat of wild animals or elephant poachers—who could be as cruel as the rebels—and caring for an infant in the wild could also seem like a death threat to mother and child. Life in the camp seemed the only choice for survival.

For many of the young girls who were rescued and returned to their villages, it was not always an easy transition. They faced stigma and shame. Often their tribal culture did not see them as victims or survivors, but as young women who had become sexually active and lost their innocence. Shame kept these girls from returning to their education. Finding a husband was nearly impossible, as it was difficult for the men to forget that the girls had once been sex slaves. For the young woman who returned with a baby, impregnated by a rebel, there was no hope of finding a husband willing to raise another man's child.

Children who return to find they have lost their families during the raids face a life of living off the street, scavenging for food, or working as a prostitute to stay alive. Vocational training may become their only hope. For thousands it meant returning to a village with no parents or family left to shelter and feed them. They were on their own, fighting once again for survival.

I traveled several times over the next six years to Kapchorwa and other areas of Uganda, continuing to promote vocational programs and developing relationships with women. With each trip I continued the education of the women I worked with and heard their stories. I learned from these women as well, eager to understand their ways of living a humble village life and honoring their culture.

On one of these trips to a refugee farm in Masindi, I tried to lift a jerry can of water to carry on my head like the women of Africa do. These cans can weigh up to fifty pounds. As a tall woman, I was amazed when I couldn't even lift it past my waist. The women poured a small amount of the water out, and I was still unable to lift it above my shoulders. After pouring out even more water, I was finally able, with their help, to place it onto my head. I took one step with the can precariously balanced and quickly lowered it for fear of damaging my neck. The women laughed as they watched my endeavors. They told me that one must start training and building the neck and arm muscles at the age of five with a very small can. The cans continue to grow in size as the child does, until they can accomplish this feat.

On another occasion I noticed a young girl of about seven struggling up a hill with a large basket of vegetables on her head. I took the basket from this young girl, not realizing the weight. My arms were spent as we reached her home at the top of the hill. Her mother greeted me with much appreciation for relieving her daughter of the burden. I could never imagine sending one of my granddaughters of the same age on this task, or that they could even manage to carry the weight.

4

## GULU

In 2013, my telephone rang and a warm friendly voice asked if I was Janet Storton, "the woman who works in Uganda teaching quilting and vocational skills to women."

I said I was.

She introduced herself as Shirley Moran from Grove Community Church in Riverside, California. She further explained that her church had partnered with a church in Gulu, Uganda. Her pastor, Tom Lance, had found the Sisters of the Heart Foundation website and said, "Here is a woman doing what we should bring to the women of Gulu." Many uneducated women attended the church in Gulu, mostly from the Acholi tribe. Shirley asked if I would be willing to travel there with her. She wanted me to help set in motion a vocational program similar to the one I had started in Kapchorwa.

I had visited the area of Gulu and read many reports and books about the Acholi tribe and the devastation that occurred to the people living in the path of the Lord's Resistance Army. It was without hesitation I agreed to help, once again feeling I was being led to give a helping hand to another group of women.

After a meeting with Shirley, in California, I knew this was meant to be; both of us felt God had brought us together. Her heart was full of love for the women she met on a prior trip to Gulu with her church. She was anxious to return to teach quilting skills. Shirley had similar thoughts to mine; maybe we would be teaching only a handful of women, but for us it was enough.

A trip was planned for the spring of 2014. Traveling together, we would bring sewing supplies, fabric, and hopefully the healing touch that sewing could provide to the souls of Gulu. Perhaps the skill would bring hope of recovery to those still traumatized by this senseless war.

Shirley and I brainstormed fundraising ideas to help provide the money needed for this mission trip. With some of my suggestions, a quilt to raffle, yard sales, and donations, she had the money raised quickly. I have learned over the years, when God designs a plan, He provides.

We met at the Seattle airport the morning of our departure. It was an excited Shirley Moran who stepped onto the airplane with me, a day and a half journey away from Uganda, halfway around the world.

Shirley and I arrived in Gulu in March of 2014. Shirley was told there would be sewing machines. When we arrived, we had a class of just over twenty students and five nonfunctioning treadle machines. Years of neglect, moisture, and dust had damaged them.

Even after coming so far, we were not discouraged. We taught them as our ancestors had learned, with a needle and thread. They cut fabric into strips and then rejoined them in a pattern, creating table mats. This was the first step to learning a craft that they could one day sell in the market place. This would be a way of raising funds to assist in supporting themselves and their families.

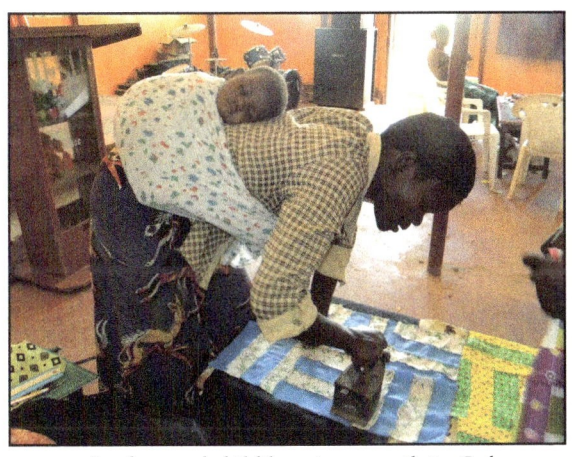

*Student and child learning to quilt in Gulu*

While teaching in Gulu, I walked into town for supplies with one of the young ladies in our class. I came to a block of long identical low concrete houses surrounded by a chain link fence. When I noticed women sitting outside the rows of doors, I asked the student if this was a prison.

She informed me it was a home for women with HIV, most of them coming from the rebel camps. Ostracized by their community and families, they had no home to go to. They were being kept there to stem the disease and keep others out. It seemed to me the same as being in a prison.

# 5

# MEETING STELLA

In my working with the women of Africa, I see them finding a sense of pride. With their accomplishments, a healing begins, sewing up their souls. Some of the rescued women keep the trauma buried inside. For many, sewing is often therapeutic; a creative outlet, having a calming effect during a time of stress or anxiety.

I am always amazed after watching the African women learn to sew, that small pieces of fabric, cut and sewn back together can have the power of uplifting the human spirit.

After years of poverty and lack of education, new skills empower them to conquer their humble and shy demeanors.

The African culture has, for centuries, beaten back women to be silent and kept in the background. Yet they work harder than most of the world's women. I heard it said, "Africa was built on the backs of the women." After being there, living and working with them, I believe this to be true.

*An uplifted spirit learning to quilt*

During the first class that Shirley and I held in Gulu, there were about twenty women and a few men of all different ages. After working awhile with the women, I was suddenly inspired to ask, "Were any of you abducted by the LRA?"

Many hands went up in the air.

My heart lurched! I was surprised by the number of raised hands. I hadn't realized so many in the room had suffered under rebel atrocities. I was once again surrounded by women who had experienced captivity by rebels and had stories of abuse and torture pinned deep inside.

That night while lying awake, I thought about those upraised hands, and knew what I needed to do. I'd heard a few of the stories from women before, but this time I knew that I needed to share their story with others.

When the class started the next morning, I happened to look up as Stella entered the room. The morning sunlight shone through the doorway as she entered, casting a warm glow behind her. I remembered the day before that she had slowly raised her hand.

Feeling drawn to her, I went over and asked if I could hear her story. She looked up at me with a blank look. It took her a moment to understand the words I asked her. I was worried perhaps I had overstepped, and it would bring back memories she had buried inside.

When someone whispered in her ear, translating my words to help her understand, she nodded her head "yes." She stood up shyly and we moved to a quiet corner, away from the other women.

I realized she spoke very little English. I asked Evelyn, a pastor to the women at this church, to interpret for me. I thought Stella would feel more comfortable talking to me with this woman and friend at her side.

With my notebook and pen in hand, I started asking questions. There was so much I wanted to learn from

Stella's experience and was hoping to hear every detail.

Her answers and her story were all too familiar. When I had stayed at a refugee farm and in other towns and villages, I'd listened to some of the horrors these young girls and boys experienced. They were forced into an imprisonment of the worst kind

As I continued to ask for details of the event, she became more explicit with the information and very willing to answer. Her demeanor and tone in her voice began to rise as she described the suffering, angered by some of the memories. I realized, here was a victim sitting next to me, pouring out the pain, the trauma, and the horrendous details of an event a fifteen year old young girl should never have to endure.

As she continued talking to me in her Luo language, with Evelyn interpreting, I could see she was having a cathartic moment, sharing the details of her story without hesitation. After many pages of notes, I felt enough questions were answered. I promised Stella that I would tell her story. To the best of my ability, based on my notes, I have recreated her account as follows.

# STELLA'S STORY

## The Raid Begins

Lightning bolts collided again and again in the distance. Thunder rolled across the plains, shaking the grass roof above me. I curled close to my sisters on the hard earth floor with only a woven mat underneath and a thin sheet over me to ward off the cold, damp air.

As the thunder grew louder, I was snapped from my dreams and sat up to listen. I began to hear voices, cackling, and war chanting, as the trucks came bounding into my village of Bobi. I peeked out to see rebels waving rifles in the air, and knew they had only death and lust on their minds. When the trucks came to a roaring stop, rebels leaped out of the trucks and began firing into the pitch black sky, ready to begin their rampage. I bolted from my hut knowing the dreaded night raiders had come.

Gunfire signaled to the foot soldiers of this cruel army who waited in hiding. Earlier that evening they slithered through the overgrowth outside our compounds. The members of the army stayed hidden, waiting until most of the men in the village were asleep and their weapons were out of reach. Older members and officers of the rebel force arriving in the trucks would start the charge. With the sound of gunfire, they ran into the compounds to begin their satanic attack of raping, looting, and murdering, while we trembled in hiding.

I was the firstborn and oldest child at the age of fifteen. My mother and I had gone over the plan many times, and I knew what I must do. With my younger brothers and sisters in tow, I ran out of our sleeping hut and into the bush. I told them to crouch low in the bushes. I begged them to lie still, not to cry, or make a noise that might give away our place of hiding. I could hear screams from the women and other girls and boys living in our small village.

I raised my head as I heard someone running close by. When a flash of lightning illuminated the sky, I saw my uncle heading towards the tall trees. A shot rang out in his direction. I cried out in anguish as I saw him fall, the bullet killing him instantly. I loved this uncle as I loved my own father and a soft wail grew in my throat. I heard rebels approaching and realized I had alerted them to our presence. What had I done? I quickly shooed my younger brothers and sisters to another bush, staying where I was as a decoy. I would be a sacrifice for their safety.

I felt a harsh tug on my arm as I was hauled off the ground by one of the rebels and pushed towards the village with such force that I stumbled, only to be jerked up and pushed again. Fearing now for my life, I went as quickly as I could back to the compound. There I saw many of my friends that had been caught, all sitting on the ground in a small tight circle, shaking in fear. Thrown to the ground beside the others, I was told not to make a sound as the rebels continued their looting of our meager rations of food; including a few goats and chickens they found belonging to the villagers.

Random shots in the darkness caused me to begin praying for my parents, hoping they had not been killed as my uncle had. Perhaps they had escaped and were hiding along with my siblings. Perhaps they were there protecting them.

It seemed like hours sitting on the damp earth, fearing the unknown. Many of my aunties had told the stories of the evil acts that happened to the ones abducted, of the suffering that occurred for those seized by these possessed men. My whole body was shaking as I realized I was now to become one of their captives and a part of the stories.

At last the gunfire stopped. My group was surrounded by the rebels, and commands were being barked at us to stand and carry all the pilfered belongings of my village. I noticed that some of the rebels looked as young as me and even younger. My breathing was of relief that my younger brothers had not been found. A large heavy jerry can of cooking oil was shoved at me to pick up and carry, as the command to start walking was given. I placed it on my head.

Hoeing furrows in the fields gave me the strength in my arms to carry the burden of the heavy oil. I am strong from years of hard labor on our farm and am able to do work most fifteen year old girls who grow up in the city will never learn. But after lifting the jerry can of oil on my head, I knew my muscles would grow weary of this weight, even as physically strong as I am.

## The Long Walk

As I began walking, burdened with the load on my head, I thought of my father who was the pastor of our village church. I attended Sunday services under a large tree that sheltered our church for as long as I could remember. My father taught me to pray and believe there was a God looking over us. It was on the terrifying night of 2003, I would question for the first time in my fifteen years if my father was preaching the truth. Did God truly exist? Was He watching over me?

When the trucks were loaded with the officers and stolen livestock, they tore out of the village making their way to the designated camp. The rest of the rebels and all of us held as captives were left to start the long and torturous journey on foot.

We were forced to begin walking on the well-worn goat paths toward the southwest, wearing what little sleeping clothes we had on and barefoot. They kept us off the main road where we would not be seen, in case any possible patrolling military might come to our aid.

The Ugandan Army routinely sent troops down these main roads to oversee the hundreds of us children who left our villages in the early evenings, walking sometimes up to ten miles into Gulu town. We would walk to sleep in the bus station, the post office, or churches where we could rest in peace and feel safe at night.

On the day of the attack, weary from a hard day of working the soil, and planting the seeds for the new harvest, most of the families of my village decided to stay together, letting us rest at home. What would one night hurt?

Through the darkness, I could see there were around twenty captives from the village, including young boys, girls, some older and some younger, but none of our parents. They were left behind to mourn the abduction of their children. Fearing a reprisal and without uttering a word or complaint, we walked all night long and into most of the next day, before reaching their camp. We walked to near exhaustion, arms and legs cramping from the weight we were carrying. My bare feet were now sore and bleeding from the miles of rocky and potholed roads we traveled on.

After many hours, I did not know how I could put one foot in front of the other. I prayed with every step to keep going. I knew if I fell, fainted, or spilled one drop of the precious oil, I would be shot or mutilated by one of the young boys as my punishment. Sometimes they would make one of the other captives do this horrific deed as a rite of initiation. They would intimidate the one chosen to do this hateful act by holding a rifle to their heads or telling them they would return to annihilate their entire family. If mutilation was the victim's fate, they would have their lips or ears cut off. I prayed for God to listen to my silent cry, bringing me rest and comfort.

It was late into the next morning before the rebels stopped our march through the forest. After coming to a small clearing sheltered by towering trees, they commanded us to put down whatever stolen goods we were carrying and help set up camp. Before there was any respite for our weary bodies, all of the girls were lined up to be sorted into two groups. The older chocolate-colored girls were sent to one side, and the darker to the other. I was sent to the dark side. Once the groups were formed, we were huddled together on the ground. Toilet breaks were given sparingly behind a bush and always under the watchful eye of a rebel. Vanity and privacy was out of the question. We were given none.

We were told that if we were caught talking together, even a whisper of a word, we would be immediately shot. Communication among us was considered to be plans in progress of an escape.

Hungry and thirsty from the long night and day of walking, we were finally given a small cup of beans that were still hard and firm with little juice. At home I was used to having the chapatti flat bread my mother made to soak up the rich broth from the beans we would cook on our farm. I would help my mother cut up onions and tomatoes, and sometimes garlic when we found it in season, to cook with the beans, adding to the flavor. The small cup of bland boiled beans would be all we were given to eat. There would be no other kind of food for months for me and the others abducted that night. No chapatti, rice, or my mother's goat stew that I love, that she cooks on special occasions. Only firm beans, undercooked and dry.

We could smell the food from the looted villages as it was cooking for the soldiers and their wives. Often we smelled chickens that were boiled, plucked and then roasted over the wood fire. We were tantalized with the aroma of roasted goat with rice or potatoes. But as usual, all we captives were given to eat, were beans, once in the morning and again at night.

Besides feeling the constant pangs of hunger, my throat was dry and parched. I suffered from continual thirst during the heat of the day. There was no water provided that first day. I sat on the hard ground praying for the rain to come. Once the skies opened with the life giving water, we tilted our heads upward with open mouths, or lapped the water from cupped hands. Occasionally, when the downpour came beating against our skin, and we were close enough to a leaf covered tree or bush, we would pick the largest leaf we could find, cup it towards the sky and slide the water from the leaf into our mouths.

But the rains usually occurred late in the afternoon, making the heat of the midday torturous. If we were lucky enough to find a pothole filled with a small amount of rain from the night before, we would fall to our knees, cupping the precious water into our mouths for some relief. We did not mind the dirt or insects mingling with the water.

## Life as a Captive

Each day the continuous walking from 6:00 a.m. until 6:00 p.m. and the carrying of heavy food items or oil was my burden. We were on the perpetual move to keep from being followed or found by rescuers. After many days and miles of walking, we reached the Rabongo Forest to the west, close to a game reserve. At night I could hear the roar of lions or the laugh of hyenas, and I worried one would come into the camp to steal me away for its meal. At times I thought this would end my suffering at last.

For months the rebels kept us among the bush and forests, on an endless migration, changing camps daily. All of us abducted girls slept in a group at night, on the harsh ground, without a blanket or extra clothing given to ward off the cold nights. Our bodies shivered, at times soaked by the torrential rain. We were living like wild animals, roaming the forests, always on the alert for death to come stalking us down.

One day I saw a rebel race towards a small group of the young boys that had been taken with me from my village. I saw him aim his rifle at one boy, heard the loud crack of it being fired, and the red blood spurting out of the boy's head as he dropped to the ground. The rebel made it clear to all of us abducted, screeching as he yelled, "This boy was talking. He was planning his escape. Now he is dead!" Of course he could not have known what the boy was trying to say, whether it was a plea for food and water, or a plan to run. He was shot without questions or hearing what he had to say. I was afraid to cry out, wanting to scream with all my soul, railing against this horrible execution. I kept my grief deep inside knowing any sound would bring me the same punishment I had just witnessed. The girls around me and I remained silent, distraught, and even more worried now that we might never see our families again. Would my fate be to live like this until I died?

With the constant movement from camp to camp, other horrors of survival had to be endured by all of us. For us girls, when we reached the time of our menstrual cycle, when the blood would run from our bodies, we were not given the usual cleaning cloths to stem the flow of blood streaming down our legs. The cramping that flowed with the blood was tolerated, and the only means of cleansing ourselves was welcomed when we came across a fetid pool of stagnant water.

Not being able to drink this water, it was used to wash the caked blood from our legs and feet. I would have to lie in a pool of menstrual blood throughout the night until daylight came and with the help of grasses remove what I could.

It was at night that the fear of being selected, grabbed by the arm and drug into the bush at gunpoint for the pleasure of a rebel, became our greatest nightmare. Girls who became pregnant would be given no medical attention or forgiveness of work during this condition. When labor began, they would only be given the aid of another of the women who had experienced giving birth themselves. Nurses or midwives to assist and insure a safe delivery were unavailable. If the pains of labor continued for too long, the young woman was left with only the shade from a tree for relief. She would have to fend for herself and catch up with the rest of the group after the baby was delivered. Occasionally a soldier would be left, watching over her to make sure she and the infant returned.

After months of living this horrendous life as a camp slave, I noticed one day there was more activity than usual in the camp. The rebels seemed to be planning an event. Food was being prepared, we were told to separate ourselves into our dark and light groups, and the usual call to stand and walk the miles we did each day halted. I heard the motorcade of the old and battered trucks first, jolting and squealing down the potholed roads. Then came the whispers from the guards telling everyone to be ready. "He is coming." It was Joseph Kony, the self-proclaimed "spirit medium" and the leader of this misfit and rabble army, coming to inspect the latest spoils of their raiding parties.

Standing in rows, all of us new girls were pushed to the ground on our knees, told to bow as he came into the camp, and ordered not to look up at his face. After walking up and down, looking at our bodies and color, he was given a chair to sit under the trees to further inspect the new camp slaves and decide which ones he would select to become his new brides.

He focused his attentions on the prettier girls who showed signs of cleverness and strength. I knew I was strong, and decided I would not speak if he spoke to me first. I would not let him know that I was taught by my father many things. I fit the categories except I was among the dark skinned girls. Dark colored and young, I could only pray I was not selected. It was a great relief when he asked for the lighter toned girls to be brought to him.

He preferred the lighter, even though his skin was dark and weathered from the years of living in the jungle. His eyes were yellow, bloodshot, and sunken from the scourge of drugs, malaria, and drinking home brew. The girls that were chosen were forced to surrender themselves to this manic servant of evil. I was grateful for the first time since my capture, and thankful that my family had the darker pigmentation that kept me safe from this monster, for now.

After the selection process, the chosen girls were taken to his side and new orders were given. Kony decided the camp would begin a new long and deadly march to South Sudan. He was trying to hide the fact that he feared the reprisals of being caught by the Ugandan military that were pushing their way towards the camps once again.

With this new command of going on a long death march, I knew with my aching muscles, sore and blistered feet, that I would die along the way—not able to walk that far. Many of the other girls felt the same way. For the first time in months, some of the abducted girls gave way to their hysteria and broke their silence with screams and crying in despair. We all knew that some of us would find it difficult to survive such a trek under the conditions we were forced to endure. The wailing in our native tongue continued, growing louder. I decided, without fear of being shot or beaten, I would join in, releasing the horror of my captivity and pent up fears to the night. I thought the louder I cried out, the sooner God would hear my pain.

Kony, I think weary of the frantic noise, afraid it might be heard if the military happened into the area, or perhaps because he was eager to get on with his new brides, gave an unusual command to release us rather than lining us up to be shot. He shouted out to the officers, "Send them back to their villages!" He already selected the ones he wanted from our group. More girls could be found and captured along the way to new camps in South Sudan. We had become hysterical. We were dirty and tired and would only slow them down. I was stunned by this reprieve, and it renewed my faith and belief in my father's teachings. Surely God finally heard my prayers and was giving me back my freedom.

A gunshot into the air silenced us to hear their new orders. Without being given food or provisions of any kind, we were told to leave the camp in our tattered and bedraggled state and start the long walk, hundreds of miles, back to our homes and our freedom.

## Rescued!

In a dazed state of unbelief, we stood and began to creep away. Fearful of rifles being aimed at our hearts, we silently, step by step, slowly backed away from our captors.

We stayed close together. I was comforted with the number of girls, as we walked the direction we believed was to the north and our way home. For days we ate very little, eating only leaves and an occasional root we would find and dig up. One time we each took a handful of dirt and swallowed what we could, just to fill our stomachs, and drank the rainwater from the potholes.

We were miles away from any other villages, as most of the people in the area were moved to the Internally Displaced Persons (IDP) Camps. Even when coming across an abandoned hut, we could find nothing left to eat, only shelter for the night. We continued walking for days, silent after so many months of not being allowed to talk. Only occasionally we would whisper to each other when we needed to stop for a rest or to look for water. We had to keep an eye out for poachers, who were as depraved as the rebels. We did not want to walk into another of the rebel camps, so we kept constantly on guard.

We finally came to a military base one evening. One of the girls had remembered going there with relatives to visit her uncle and gave us hope of finding it. We were the walking dead when we arrived at this base. Only Mother Nature and our prayers to God had kept us alive. We put our hands up in the air, frightened and exhausted as we walked towards the front gate. If we were mistaken as the rebel enemy by our bedraggled state and worn clothes, our freedom and escape from the camp would be in vain. We were afraid the guards would begin shooting us on sight.

We surrendered to the front gate security, and told them our story. Fortunately, they believed us and took us into the compound for food and rest. Tears of joy began streaking down our faces, washing the red soil down our cheeks and we began hugging in disbelief that our rescue had come. The nightmare over, we were going home!

As I saw the red mud on our faces, mingled with our tears, I thought of the saying in my homeland, "The dirt is red from all the years of bloodshed."

A call was sent out to World Vision Headquarters in Gulu. They were told an Acholi group of abducted girls had escaped and were alive. A truck from World Vision would come to the military base to pick us up and bring us back to the city for relocation and reunion with any of our families that survived the raids. We were afraid when we returned home that some of us would discover none of our family members were alive, and we would have to struggle for survival once again.

Waiting for the truck to arrive, they provided us with hot water to bathe. We could finally scrub off layers of dirt from our bodies. We rinsed the parasites out of our hair that had grown long and stringy. It was a challenge trying to remove the pests that had burrowed under our skin for months. They brought some T-shirts and pants they rounded up for us to put on; replacing the ragged clothing that was so shredded and torn it barely covered our bodies.

They took us into the dining hall and provided us with a meal. I thought this was a feast for us starving girls like I had never seen before. Bowls of hot steaming rice, round Irish potatoes cooked in a pot of oil, chicken pieces stewed with tomatoes, chapatti to scoop up the chicken and rice, and the necessary malaquan greens to give us the desperately needed vitamins were set down on a table for us to eat. Plates of sliced banana and mangos were placed on the table to finish our meal.

No more scooping up beans with my dirty, blistered hands. We all began shoving the food into our mouths, not believing after so many months the food would taste so good. Drinking clean water and drinking sweetened tea became a new luxury.

After filling our stomachs, we were taken into a meeting room for a debriefing. I gave what little information I could about the location of the camps and the treatment I experienced. Shame filled my mind as I described my capture. I kept many of the details within my own memory. Tears kept flowing as I described what I could from my life in the camps and the overwhelming relief that I was now free and on my way home.

Feeling human again, I waited in the World Vision holding room not knowing if my father, Frances Oweka, was even alive. How could I continue surviving, even now, if I lost my entire family that night death came to our farm? The trauma I endured over the last six months kept me reticent to hope and my heart racing.

I saw him first as he entered the room full of the other girls who had hopes their parents would come. I was overwhelmed with joy. My father was alive and here to find me! I stood and shouted out to him, "Father, I am here!" Hearing my call, he rushed towards me. He reached out and held me like he hadn't since I was a young girl. Together we hit the floor in an embrace, as my father began giving thanks to the Lord for saving his most beloved girl! He prayed mightily with his grateful appreciation for the Lord's protection over me and returning me safely home. It was only by God's grace I had been delivered back to him from the rebels.

## Going Home

It was another long walk from Gulu to our home in Bobi. But this time I was not told to be silent, I was given water when I was thirsty, I was not carrying heavy provisions, and I had my father alongside of me for protection.

My mother, who had stayed home to have a meal ready to celebrate my return, kept a watchful eye on the road. She told me she was impatiently pacing, waiting to see us arrive home. When she saw our two tall figures walking towards the family compound, she dropped the bag of tea in her hands and ran to the road. I saw my mother running towards us and then fall to her knees in the dirt wailing and lifting her hands to the sky, giving praise for bringing me, her first and oldest girl child, home. My mother, Margaret Lamumu, cried out with a heartwarming blessing, seeing that her daughter was saved. She could not believe her luck, but believed in her God. I ran to where my mother was kneeling in the dirt. I wept tears of relief, releasing the pain I held inside for so many months, as I also fell to the earth and into my mother's arms.

8

# THE HEALING BEGINS

When Stella finished her story, I asked her to stand. I wrapped her in an embrace, wanting to erase the pain of that time in her life, not wanting to let her go.

She melted into my arms with relief from telling her story to someone who wanted to know. I had heard the pain in her words and knew I needed to share it with others. I wanted to bring awareness of her plight and that of thousands like her.

However, I was also worried her reliving the memories would disrupt the joy she had found in the class. I asked Stella how she felt about learning to sew, and what this could mean to her future. Her smile lit up the room. She answered in limited English, "Learning to sew is making me very happy!" I hadn't realized this young woman had dimples until now—an unusual feature in African women—and how cavernous these dimples would appear since I had never seen her smile. It was fortunate Joseph Kony had not seen Stella smile.

Strong, beautiful, and clever, if it were not for his preference for lighter colored skin, she may never have been released.

*Stella, strong and clever, smiling*

At 24 years old now, Stella is past the marrying age. She lives at home with her parents, working in the fields and cultivating the land to provide food for the family. She is content to live her life helping her family and members of their church. Her family has moved closer to Gulu where she attends church and is part of the women's ministry. She finds comfort and healing in her faith. She is eager to continue learning to sew. She wants to become proficient enough to sell the items she makes in the marketplace to the tourists and NGOs (Non Governmental Organizations) traveling to Gulu. Many of these organizations and mission groups come to the north, helping repair the hearts and minds of so many children who suffered during this war.

It was a sad departure when we left Gulu. I said my goodbyes to this wonderful new group of women and men that I had met.

*Shirley Moran with class in Gulu*

Then a long goodbye to Stella. She seemed sad that I was leaving. I knew in my heart I would return and see her again one day.

We had an all day drive to the village of Kapchorwa. We hired a driver who would safely get us there. As we were driving through a rural farming village, I noticed a sign that read "Bobi," the village from which Stella had been abducted. With the story fresh in my mind, I leaped up from the back seat and asked the driver to stop. Armed with my camera, I jumped out. I wanted to see and remember this village that had been under attack on that dreadful night, as were so many others along our route. I wanted to know where Stella and her family had their farm.

This was Bobi, the home of the Acholi tribe. The people living here were subsistence farmers whose homes and small farms spread across the savannah of northern Uganda. Typical of other rural villages in Uganda, the Acholi live in round huts constructed in the waddle and daub style; framed with tree branches and wall components consisting of mud, stones, and cow dung. Grasses or banana leaves form a thatched roof, and dirt is hardened on the floors by vigorous pounding. The Ugandan tribes have built their homes this way for thousands of years, finding the local building materials the cheapest form of construction. The sleeping huts are usually 10 feet in diameter, and a bit larger for the cooking and storage units. Women sweep the dirt daily between the huts that are huddled together in African communal style. They live in dirt, surrounded by mud walls, but most farming women take pride in the small amount of land they have.

Stella was the oldest of three girls and two boys in this small compound. Her sleeping hut would have been bare except for a thin handmade rope of papyrus reeds tied across a small section holding what little clothes she owned, including a school uniform. Often a small rustic table from the local carpenter's shop will sit against the wall to hold the well-worn and tattered Bible, a school book, or the occasionally used kerosene lantern when they could afford the fuel. Other small huts were built beside the children's sleeping hut for the parents and additional members of the family, all living together in a unit for protection.

Their cooking was done outside, unless it was the rainy season. Then a small charcoal burner was brought inside to cook their simple meals, creating an aroma of smoke and wet earth that permeated the air.

Every inch of soil around the perimeter of the small compound is planted with maize, beans, cassava, peas, a few fruit trees of bananas, papayas, mangoes, and malaquan greens they depend on for its rich supply of iron in their diet. The villagers sell excess produce in order to buy other necessities, such as flour, rice, cooking oil, soap, tea, and sugar. Money for school fees, uniforms, and other supplies is difficult for these poor farmers to afford. For most families, only the oldest children are sent to school and usually just the boy child.

The LRA rebels found raiding the small farmers for their provisions prevented them from having to farm for themselves. This enabled them to stay on the move. Since 1986 Joseph Kony and his ragtag rebel army of misfit drug-induced boy soldiers have murdered, tortured, and mutilated their way through these northern villages of Uganda. In Bobi, Stella and her family were in their deadly path. Kony's rebels continue to devastate the villages of northeastern Africa.

*Bobi hut*

## HOME IN SISTERS

Africa has changed my core and being. I relish my time spent in the villages of Uganda and the relationships I have made with the people living there. When I leave my comfortable home before each trip, I leave the luxuries of America to live life in a primitive fashion, reminiscent of the lifestyle of my homesteading grandparents, ranching in Wyoming in similar conditions.

For most visitors, a trip to Africa is going on safari to spot and photograph animals in the wild. For me, I have found so much more. At times it means dealing with biblical rain storms, dirt and mosquitoes, cold showers and many inconveniences, and yet, Africa has captured my heart. I am lured back again and again by the people, their unremitting spirits, the majestic vistas, and by listening to where He leads.

Karen Blixen, author of *Out of Africa*, must have felt the same love while starting her coffee farm in Kenya. Dennis Finch Hatten and Beryl Markham, both famous African aviators, must have experienced it soaring over the Serengeti in their airplanes. Bror Blixen found it as a safari guide. Joan and Allan Root shared their passion through photographing it. Ernest Hemmingway wrote about it, mesmerized with its beauty. Even after crashing his small airplane and spending the night along the crocodile and hippopotamus infested Nile River, waiting to be rescued, he continued returning.

Africa holds some of us in an infectious grasp, like malaria. With the right medical prevention, malaria can be cured...but you will never be rid of it. For some, this love is like a jungle vine wrapping its fast growing tentacles around your heart. Until you have walked the goat paths with women as they recall ancient stories of their ancestors, worked on a farm feeling the warmth of the equatorial sun on your back, watched the mango colored sunsets and the dark skies of night light up with the thunderous lightning storms in the distant valley, you have not experienced this land. Africa is like a quilt. Bits and pieces of the fabric of life, cut and sewn together...the good, the evil, the sacred, the corrupt, the tamed, and the wild, all patch-worked together, creating a "blanket of color."

There are always the horrific crimes, corruption, and sad stories of tortured souls like this of Stella and others. But I can't let that stop me from coming back; giving what little hope I can to amend for the evil that infests this continent. I cannot turn my back on the needs of the women and children because of the few discomforts I experience along the way. Eating rice, beans, and cabbage for a month humbles me to profound gratitude when I go home.

I am overwhelmed with the beauty I find in Africa. The terrain more extraordinary than any other in the world I have visited. Green and lush in some areas and then arid and dry in others. A conflicting scene that keeps me wondering what is around the next bend in the road. Traveling through the farming villages, it seems I have gone back a hundred years to an era of living off the land, a primitive life, neighbor helping neighbor, donkeys still being used to carry heavy loads. I feel I am in an ancient place and time, living when life was hard, but simple. America has advanced so far into the computer and social media age, yet in African villages, it seems time has stood still.

For people living in poverty, surrounded by nature's beauty, happiness is found in a rainstorm producing the growth of their crops. Their needs are few, having food to feed the children each day is enough. They are happy with simple pleasures, taking life slower; as if they are savoring every precious moment they have in this place.

The goodness I find here surpasses the challenges. While in the mountains of this country, I often reflect on my day, sitting next to a waterfall with a cup of home grown, fire roasted and freshly ground coffee, listening to birds chirping and monkeys chattering in the trees. These are moments of great peace. Here I can forget the worries and fast pace of life in America, and I live like the

Africans, and just breathe.

*View from Janet's hut in Kapchorwa*

I am humbled by the strength of the African women on every visit, and the appreciation I am shown for the smallest effort or gift. They are eager to learn any new task, whether it be sewing, cooking, child care, or proper sanitation. The village women have lived their lives working the soil on their knees in the dirt. They believe it is with new skills they will rise up and become empowered with the hope of a better life.

In Kapchorwa, almost all of the women survive as sustainable farmers. I find that these amazing women live with very little in material wealth. Yet they are rich in their souls with the love they have for God, their families, and each other. This I would also find is true of the Acholi women living in the northern region of Uganda.

Twice a year I return, teaching vocational skills on refugee farms, at orphanages, or in vocational schools to the women and young girls of Uganda. I leave Africa with as much learned from the women as I am there to teach. Their life experiences humble me.

Exhausted and fragile after every trip, I can be found weeping in the produce department of the grocery store, feeling guilty over the bountiful selection. We don't wait for the seasonal produce to arrive, nor do we break our backs digging the furrows, planting the seeds, worrying if the rains will come during the growing season, harvesting the food, or cooking it to keep our families alive.

I used to complain about the price of a pound of specialty coffee. After spending a few days working on coffee farms with women farmers, watching for snakes as we work our way around the trees in the mud, picking the cherries until my fingers are red and raw, lifting the heavy gunny sack sized bags onto their heads, bags so heavy I am worried of damage to my neck if I try, working until dusk when my legs can hardly carry me home, I now preach, "We don't pay enough!"

Guilt engulfs me as I drive my car to town running errands. In Uganda we walk miles each day accomplishing the simple tasks of daily living, rain or shine. We walk the distance going to church, or walk to check on a child or woman that is ill. I have walked miles with a woman in early stages of labor to the clinic of the midwife. In the village of Kapchorwa, where our Foundation for Empowering Women is established, I have walked the mountainsides with the members looking for the neediest, giving them the financial assistance to help through a crisis. These women have been an inspiration to my life and a witness to the Christian community. Always moving forward, backwards never!

*Kapchora women cooking*

Stella, strong and clever, has inspired me. She experienced the worst life has to offer and endured the pain of being held captive. She was tortured with exhaustion, hunger, and thirst, yet she did not give up hope or her God, and she made it home. Remembering her story will always keep me strong, no matter what life brings my way. I am the lucky one, waiting for His timing, and riding the wind to where He wants me to be.

*"I can do all things through Christ who strengthens me."*

*Philippians 4:13*

## UGANDAN HISTORY

Uganda has endured political unrest, repression, and terror under the cruel presidencies of Idi Amin (1971-1979), and Milton Obote (1966-1970 and 1980-1985). When Yoweri Museveni, a military leader who helped overthrow Amin and Obote, seized power in 1985, he promised to bring back peace to his nation.

Unfortunately, the people in the North and especially the Acholi tribe, who had been grievously oppressed by the former governments, have little hope for the future under the new president.

Across the northern savannah of Uganda, at the borders of South Sudan, arose a woman named Alice Lakwena. A member of the northern Acholi tribe, she started the Holy Spirit Movement in opposition to the new president Yoweri Museveni in 1986. Tired of the oppression of her tribe under the former presidents, she decided to rise against the new president, doubting Museveni's desire to finally unite the people of Uganda.

She forged alliances with other rebel militia groups and marched towards the capital city of Kampala with the intention of taking over the government and freeing the northern tribes from any government rule.

She convinced her supporters that spirits were

channeling through her to lead this movement to take over the leadership of the north. This effort was short-lived. She was captured and exiled before reaching the city.

Joseph Kony, claiming to be a distant cousin to Alice, assumed the role of leader to the remnants of Alice's army, renaming the force the Lord's Resistance Army. This self-imposed warlord was able to recruit thugs and thieves and amassed one of the most treacherous rebel groups ever formed. With Kony's leadership, they scoured rural villages throughout the countryside, kidnapping, raiding, pillaging, and causing death and destruction along their path. Kony, neither an educated man nor inherently a tribal chief, has piloted this army for decades, creating the worst and longest civil war in Africa's history.

To fill ranks and increase the army's numbers, Kony started abducting young girls and boys, then stealing food to feed them all. Behaviors went out of control when drugs, home brew, and evil intentions took over this madman and his faction. What started as a band of rebels to liberate the north suddenly became a guerrilla group oppressing the north.

Kony's directive to his troops was to take food, cooking oil, clothing, and livestock. Many of the soldiers were children themselves who had been abducted in previous raids. The kidnapped boys would be trained as soldiers. The girls would cook, become porters of the stolen loot, and forcibly comfort the soldiers at night. Privileged officers selected the girls they wanted for wives without question or ceremony.

For over twenty-two years the rebels have perpetuated hideous practices, thinking they would enable Kony's twisted vision to become a reality. Kony's preposterous quest was to rule the country "in the name of the Lord," hoping to convert millions of people living in Uganda to live by the Ten Commandments, while refusing to follow the rules himself. He believed this to be his mission and convinced thousands of the need to revolt against their government, or by force, to follow him.

This long period of suffering continues today. Now, they continue their march of terror, not only in Uganda but in other parts of Africa as well.

During the beginning of Kony's activities, little attention or mention of the crimes being committed was given by world media. Where was CNN or the BBC?

It took years before any news stations alerted the Western World to the atrocities that were taking place in Uganda. In 2003, three young American men, recently graduated from college, went to Africa to make a film about the civil war in Darfur, South Sudan.

Jason Russell, Bobby Bailey, and Laren Poole were traveling through northern Uganda when they found the children of Gulu walking to town to sleep at night for their safety. The men realized they found a war right in northern Uganda affecting the lives of thousands of children. They were stunned to think that these children, laying side by side in rows head to toe, were invisible to the rest of the world.

Their award-winning documentary, *The Invisible Children*, awakened the Western World to what was happening to these night commuters in the LRA's path. Before this film was made, World Vision, one of the few entities at work in the area, called these villagers "pitied and ignored."

Kony's rebel group, the LRA, has recently been pushed out of Uganda, but continues to roam in African countries. The group also influences copycat terrorist clusters to spring to life.

# EPILOGUE

In 2005, the newly formed International Criminal Court put out their first arrest warrant. It was for Joseph Kony. He was being indicted for his crimes against humanity and war crimes. This was the first time the world took an official stand against Kony. Joseph Kony became the most wanted man in the world. A young Acholi girl named Grace Akallo, who was abducted by Kony's rebels while living in Gulu, stated after being rescued, "God was carrying me on His back when I thought I was walking by myself." She had not given up hope of returning home. Grace was a soldier girl living in the rebel camps for years, and endured the forced marches. She was taken to the United States as a speaker, giving her testimony before Congress on April 26, 2006. Finally, the United States would hear again of the atrocities of this Civil War and the fate of thousands of children in Uganda from a girl who had experienced it. She is now working for World Vision in Uganda.

No one seems to know for sure why it was taking the Ugandan military so long to capture the bands of Kony's army. Sometimes the rebels were living in different camps and split into groups that numbered in the thousands. Rumors were often heard to say that if the rebels were finally caught, there would be many of the Ugandan officers out of a job. I was in the country in 2009, and elated when a report was given that the Government forces had Kony and his declining army of 1500 surrounded in a swamp with no way out. Unfortunately, the next morning the news read they had all miraculously escaped. This development led to the rise of more rumors which were hard to dismiss.

Within the last few years, the Ugandan government launched a Peace and Development Plan, a reconstruction program for north Ugandans, tailored to train youths in vocational skills to become economically self-reliant. It is here, in the north, that young people have been the most neglected due to the war. Generations have missed out on education and training.

While still in the country in March 2014, I learned the United States government was sending an additional 150 special forces along with four CV-22 Osprey helicopters and troops to maintain and fly the aircraft on the hunt for the warlord Joseph Kony and his troops. The U.S. personnel are only authorized to "provide information, advice, and assistance" to the African union force tracking Kony and his rebels. "While combat-equipped they are prohibited from engaging the LRA forces unless in self-defense," the Washington Post reported. The children in the camps become the innocent collateral damage when attacks begin.

Escaping capture by the Ugandan military, the Rebel army fled into the Democratic Republic of the Congo, Central African Republic, and South Sudan. Several units of the rebel forces have spread across these three countries, larger than the size of the state of California. Kony continues leading his small dwindling force (information was received that numbers have dwindled to a mere 250, including captives) in constant and exhausting motion, moving from camp to camp, evading capture in the jungles of these three countries. It is reported at times they find a safe haven with Muslim extremists in South Sudan, putting Christian captives in harm's way. The LRA fighters use extreme violence, murder, mutilation, rape, and kidnapping, allowing the extremist groups to learn their techniques—raiding with copycat methods. Terrorist groups like the Boko Harram in Nigeria are imitating Kony's evil ways, believing Western education and beliefs are a sin. When Kony's numbers decrease, the abductions of boys and girls escalate.

Originating in 1986, the war that Joseph Kony waged has continued to be the longest and most brutal in Africa's history. It is estimated that over 60,000 children have been abducted to date. It is unknown how many common law wives he has taken. Some estimate it is as many as forty to more than fifty, and he has fathered countless children. While on the move between South Sudan and Central African Republic, in the first five months of 2014, he has led 65 attacks in villages, and taken at least 93 abductees. Although this is a significant decrease from years past, it is 93 too many.

The Ugandan military pursuing the rebels are 5,000 strong, with about 100 U.S. Special Forces advising them, along with soldiers from the Congo and Central African Republic. And yet Kony has still not been found. A report from the Invisible Children Organization believes, with the help of the U.S., they are closer than ever. With the additional might and technology of the Americans, I wait for the good news he has finally been captured.

Uganda once was called "The Pearl of Africa" by Winston Churchill. For over two decades the world seemed to ignore that the people were living in constant fear of attack and felt ignored and forgotten. Villagers called the rebels "demons of the night that came in the dark to snatch the innocent." Children in the villages grew up seeing people murdered and had to walk over dead bodies lying in the roadside.

Joseph Kony and his army have left Uganda for now, continuing their devastation in other countries, leaving behind a path of human spirits destroyed by their greed. The Ugandans are finding it a long and tedious journey to recovery, some never achieving it.

The grass under the elephant's feet
is being stomped, while the battles of
rebel groups rage on.

*It is the innocent in their path, left behind,
that continue to suffer.*

# SPECIAL ACKNOWLEDGMENTS

**Stella**

*I am humbled by your strength and courage to survive when most wouldn't. You increased my faith in God and to never give up the hope that is granted for those who believe. You encouraged me to write, inspiring me to tell the story so your experience and that of thousands of others would never be forgotten. Your smile lights up a room and warms my heart. The healing begins and your future appears brighter with your renewed faith and willingness to conquer the past. Keep smiling, beautiful Stella. God is smiling upon you.*

**Florence**

*You were the first to tell me the story of your captivity by the Lord's Resistance Army (LRA). I am privileged you felt comfortable with me and found an eager friend to listen to your story for the first time. I was new to Uganda and had much more to learn. Our evening around the cook fire listening to your experience into the depths of hell left me astonished that events so heartless could happen in the $21^{st}$ century. The incredible courage of your father, who walked into a rebel camp armed only with a few cows and goats for your ransom to freedom, I will never forget. The love he showed for your life and that of your unborn child has no equal. You were the first to cause my tears to fall.*

**Olive**

*Although our lives touched for only a few brief days, I have never forgotten. I told you when I had to leave I would think of you every day, and for eight years that holds true. You came to me carrying your very sick and feverish young baby boy on your back while sick with malaria yourself. After walking many miles for medical help, the desperation in your eyes that spoke to me, pleading for help to save your child, tore through my soul. Although there were hundreds in line before you, I knew God's purpose for my being there that day was to help relieve the suffering for you and your son. After you both were given the medical care needed, I wrapped your baby, Edmondo, in a new homemade quilt brought from the U.S. Your eyes were illuminated, speaking volumes of appreciation for this gift of warmth. I will never forget your parting words when you turned to ask, "How will I find you again?" We live half a world away from each other, you in a very remote village at the top of a mountain, with no phone or postal address. So far, we have not managed to find each other. But the photo of a beautiful young mother named Olive (the same as my own mother's) with a baby on her back, sits in a frame on my desk. You are not forgotten.*

**Christine**
*You sought me out and pleaded with me to return after seeing the "blankets of color" I made for my sponsor child. Little did we know or dream, I would continue returning for years. I believe in God's planning, and you and I are the tools He used to make these dreams come true. Your friendship and watchful care over me while in country is deeply appreciated. We laugh and tell each other all our troubles as only sisters can. I know in my heart when you plead once again for me to come and live in the village, so you and my other sisters can care for me during my later years of life, that not only would I be one of the luckiest of elderly women, but the most loved and cared for. Only sisters can do that for each other.*

**Sisters Of The Heart**
*You know who you all are. As our numbers grow, the pride I feel over your achievements swells beyond comprehension. From the beginning of our first workshop together, the laughter, giggles, singing, dancing, and loving sisterhood has not ceased. Your energy and compassion for others in the village is what strengthens me to keep returning. Your accomplishments and desire to work hard to make life easier for others is astonishing. You have taught me the true meaning of "it takes a village" and what working together for the sake of others signifies. Your lives humble me into wanting to do more in my own—loving more deeply. I taught you to sew, but you have taught me to "dance!"*

## Sisters of the Heart Foundation
*"Women Empowering Women,"*
continues to grow and reach out to the needy by;

Bringing Hope
Building a Future
Empowering a Community

---

Ways of helping and praying for these women can be found on our website and Facebook pages:
*sistersoftheheartfoundation.org*
*facebook.com/sistersoftheheart.org*

From the website you can purchase handmade, one of a kind items crafted from African-made fabric by the ladies of Uganda.

You can donate by contacting Janet Storton by email;
*janetstorton@gmail.com*

or by sending a check made out to:
*Sisters of the Heart*
*P.O. Box 1743*
*Sisters, Oregon 97759*

---

*Your donations will be deposited into their 501c3, a nonprofit organization. All gifts are tax deductible.*

## About Janet Storton

*Janet Storton grew up in the large naval town of National City, California, where her earliest classmates came from around the world. Through these relationships, she learned a respect for other cultures as they shared with her their various ethnic traditions. For her, global citizenship was her first nation.*

*Janet was drawn to Africa when she was only ten. Listening to a missionary couple speak at Sunday school set her heart toward service there. However, it was not until 2007, that she went on her first missions trip to Uganda. She has traveled there two or three times a year since.*

*Janet lives in Sisters, Oregon, with her husband of 44 years. There she teaches quilting and works tirelessly raising funds for the entrepreneurial programs that she has started in Uganda.*

CPSIA information can be obtained
at www.ICGtesting.com
Printed in the USA
FSOW03n0948070616
21219FS

9 780983 833376